VOLUME 9

EXPENSALISM

OBSTACLES FOR A GOVERNMENT

AT THE OTHER'S EXPENSE

FIRST EDITION

Carlos L. Partidas

quimicor2@gmail.com

DEDICATORY
For Earth's intelligent and capable human beings

CONTENTS

RECOGNITION

To all the energy that animates all the
Living Beings of the Earth

CARLOS PARTIDAS

1

EXPENSALISM

An expensalist (At the other's Expense) is one who, in order to be able to act, is nourished or lives at the expense of the ideas of others. The expensalist does not have a dogma on which to base himself, nor a form of action of his own, because he really suffers from mental dyslexia. Its basic doctrine is the expensalism. And this is a cognitive bias, which does not allow people who suffer it, to be able to see themselves. And in some cases, most of these expensalists don't even know that these problems affect us, and they just march forward because they see others doing it.

But this attitude is part of an innate character of the personality, so it's going to be very difficult for these people to discover themselves, or even for others to discover them. And this condition, of course, will be a rather complex problem to solve by means of psychological help, because it is supposed that to be able to change this suitability in a conscious way, the first step to be taken is precisely to be able to recognize oneself. But the expensalists don't do it, because they don't know that they have this cognitive bias. And by trying to talk to them, it would be like explaining to a madman the causes of his madness, because they are not going to be able to understand this.

These are a kind of people who live mentally in their own world of impossibility. They are clumsy, and they perceive the phenomena of the world, only in their own way; or as they believe that society is, but they do not contribute anything to improve it. In such a way that for them, others will always be wrong, because they believe that the world is really as they see it. They cannot be creative, but they have an astonishing ability to copy or imitate qualities from those whom they consider to be the possessors of a certain skill, which they do not have. And if they do not succeed, because they do not know how to do it, they try to acquire with the equivalent in money, the ability of others, so that these others, do the work that they are not able to do, or solve a problem that for them is complex. And they put at their disposal all the means and resources, so that whoever they consider can achieve it, feels confident and comfortable in his task, at least during the solution of the case, which for the expensalist is something extremely complex. And they always consult the experts, because they do not have the ability to channel the solution of the problem through logic. And the expensalists do not know how to approach a certain strategy.

They always present a mental incapacity, but they try not to prove it. And to everything that they consider confusing, they want to give a scientific explanation, when in some group, they catch one or one that they consider they are not going to oppose their arguments. And those scientific problems that they believe they can master correctly, they adorn their exposures with a special touch, to enhance their supposed endowments of wisdom.

And they buy the ideas from others; but once they get what they want, they kick it and threaten it so that they do not betray them, because from now on they do not want to know more about who did the work for them. And in this way, they try to erase the evidence, to demonstrate that they were the ones who contributed the idea. And they will always have to go after other experts, in order for them to be able to support themselves with their mental disability, because the expensalists are not capable of achieving things by themselves.

They are usually people who love money; and they buy the intelligence of others, because they don't even want to recognize the ability of others. Only the one they acquired with money. And in order not to recognize the capable, they invent in some way the falsehood, in some way, to harm those who really helped them to obtain their achievements.

And the expensalists are enclosing themselves in circles of power, in order not to lose their positions; or as a way of safeguarding privileges that they really do not deserve. And they proudly raise a false attitude of achievement achieved by something they have not achieved on their own. Because they act only by instinct. They are humanoids, or they would be like the transition, if they make it, between an animal and an intelligent human being.

And there are a great number of these people, because even you will have the opportunity to go and recognize them. And you will get many of them, because they are around you. But they won't be able to read this book, because for them, this book has no value. Anyway, that knowledge is also relative. And other expensalists will only see some acts and actions of other expensalists, exposing events, where great genius sprouts and is transfigured. And by means of a stupid speech, they get involved in history, but from this chronological laby- rinth they won't be able to get out, because they don't even know the first stanza of the national anthem.

The expensalists want to take advantage of others' knowledge, and copy exactly the image from others, to show themselves before others, with what they cannot achieve by themselves. And when they instruct groups, they run off to impart what others have copied, as if it were their idea. And at the same time they strategically select these groups, because those chosen by them must have less cognitive value. That is why, for the most part, expensalists often become primary school teachers. Because there are many children there, and there will be a unique opportunity to be able to give orders. But generally, very few have an end to educate or form the child.

So these people will form and participate in groups, in which there are others with a low intellectual level, because by doing so within that category, they can express what they have cop- ied from others without receiving objections. And what they copy, they can enunciate with great skill and grace, because they know that these groups of lesser intellect can flatter them and recognize them as geniuses.

But when they are in front of a more advanced group, they will keep quiet, because the expensalists know well that they would not tolerate the objections, or those questions that they will not be able to answer. Many take notes and learn them, but hide the source, because they will expose the copied idea as if it were theirs. So they do not recognize the person who emitted the idea. But it will be an idea that the expensalists will not be able to materialize, because they do not know how to do it. They learned only the idea, and, painfully for them, always behind the idea, usually has to come consequently an objective, or action that will glimpse the idea.

And to express what they have copied from others, they constrict their mouths and raise their eyebrows by throwing their heads back a little. Because the one who proposed the idea, only said it with the words that emanated from his thought, but in the background of the idea, an objective is implicit; and generally, the one who proposes an idea, or who understands a reason, is the one who knows how to carry out what is proposed.

And for the expensalists, the copied image or the idea, they manage to make it look like their own in order to be able to sustain themselves, and they feel well endowed, because perhaps they need that compliment and recognition that they cannot obtain. They tell others with amazing detail what they should do; but when that someone asks them to try to do what they propose, they don't know how to do it. And they turn again to the expert to come up with a solution, and the most certain thing is that they will not understand it either, and in this way they scratch their heads, and always live confused in their minds, without proposing an idea of their own.

So they come and go from one place to another, or to some emptiness, because they cannot or do not have the capacity to imagine, to be able to associate ideas through analytical thought. And when they have money, they will get that idea in some way, which after being acquired, they assume as their own creation, because they assigned a price to that idea. And they buy it with the equivalent value of money. And for this reason alone, the idea already belongs to them. And it's their property, because they bought it.

And many of these people come to my imagination: communal leaders, aspirants to political office, government ministers, or the reverends of a church. But they don't really know that with this attitude of expensalists, they can cause great harm to the administration of a revolution, to a church, or even to the coexistence of the human race. Because the truth is that these people unfortunately exist, and it is very difficult to discover them or discover in them those cognitive appearances.

Some and some become arrogant, that is, because they cannot execute the ideas, they retreat by fleeing forward, but not without first, they will try to damage morally and with lies to the one who can, as a way to get out of the way. And so they become false, presumptuous and evil critics.

And the expensalists are also the typical nepotists, because some occupy important positions in some ministry, and not to lose their privileges, appoint a family member, which usually has to be also an expensalist, for them to be able to send it, and thus achieve, that this relative occupies an important position, but that this position is strategic for them to be able to expand their rank of dominion. A range of influence that they cannot measure either, because they do not have the capacity to know how far that limit can go. So they practice an egoism that has no end either.

The expensalists of the high positions love it when they are flattered. They are pleased when they announce them with the fanfare of a trumpet, and you have to receive them well; and if possible, bow to them when they pass, or stand when they arrive. Because if you don't do these gestures of reverence to them, they are offended. And they are delicately tasting only a small portion of the great banquet. And the drink for them cannot be the same as that of others, because theirs has to be exclusive. And the drinks of more years, will be theirs. But when the other influential ones leave, only those of their circle of influence will remain; and among them the great drunkenness will be unleashed, and what they really are will emerge from them, because the alcoholic beverage is the only thing that manages to remove them from their self-absorption or presumption. They may even cry during the drunkenness, the frustration caused by their expensalism.

And they will try to occupy the most influential and important positions, which may not necessarily be those of a government, but also from the high position of an opposition; or for example in a church. And those below will not be equal to them, but their subjects. And thanks to that ability to hide easily or to be sneaky, they are vain; that is, they talk too much but without any sustenance. And if they work as simple mechanics of a railroad, they say that it was because of them that the whole railroad and the stations were designed and built along with the railroads. And they skilfully capture among the lower level users, to tell them that it was thanks to them that the railway exists.

But perhaps the expensalists exist, joining a list with a greater quantity of qualities, but these are worse and more dangerous than the useless ones, because it is easy to discover the useless ones because of their lack of dexterity; but not the expensalists, because they do not participate in the work directly, but they only give the orders, so that others execute them. They really do not know how to do it.

And they manage with great skill to adopt an attitude of great kindness and delicacy or sweetness in their words, before those who can assign him some important position, because with a soft voice, they easily deceive the one who grants the position. But when the one who grants them the position is absent, they begin to tell others about the weaknesses of the one who assigns the position, because they consider that he is occupying a position that he does not deserve; but that they, as expensalists can execute better this position. But the expensalists would like to occupy all the positions at the same time. Because they like to give orders so that they are faithfully obeyed. And when someone refutes them, they become furious, such as tensing and jumping with the tips of their feet and clenching their teeth and fists tightly. Their eyes are sprouted and rounded. Or they emit a thunderous tremor with their jaws; and many times they show a paleness in their face and a whiteness in their lips. And they turn gray.

And wanting to get them out of that world will be a difficult task. Because they are "as rich of towns" or arrogant; and they want to be dominant, since only they believe themselves to be the only ones, and therefore they are the ones who deserve the recognition of the others. They are louts.

But perhaps the expensalists leave a "narrow road" to enter their worlds, inasmuch as they admire those whom they see have reached a degree, which they will not be able to reach. Although later, these expensalists can occupy positions, which they will take care of jealously, so that those who have the ideas do not approach, for in the expensalists there is fear that someone more qualified than they can displace them from their positions. And that is why they remain protected by lies, because as we said they are non-basement speakers.

And in general, the expensalists can be successful in business, as they are not creators, nor do they risk much. And if the business works on its own, they won't even realize how it does it. And they pay for someone to manage them. And if the business grows and goes well, they say it's because of them. But if the business goes bad, they blame the manager. And they shout at the incapacity of the other. But also if someone manages their business with good strategies, this can generate their big fortunes, which in turn feeds them like a snowball their expensalism. And they will get a yacht; but it doesn't matter that they don't have a beach, but it has to be the best yacht, and they park it on the flat in front of their house, only to know that they have a yacht. To the delight they feel, when others see that only they can have a yacht. And they just want to have a yacht, because that gives to them a glamour.

And the expensalists only try to dominate the world market. Even if it is possible to market on the planet Mars or any planet they can think of, because they cannot discern between the real and the impossible. Well, they just want to move forward, without thinking about others, or those who have nothing, not even something to eat.

And the expensalists use any deceptive strategy to somehow create their ephemeral fortunes; and it could be through a phantom company or one that is not real. And to achieve this, they create the stock market, where they have the opportunity not to create anything but to make money. And with this, they can found an extravagance, such as an oil company that is a ghost. And this company sells oil. But the company has no oil, because they only place the shares of the ghost company on the stock market. And they do not deliver the negotiated oil, because the delivery of the such oil is for the future. But the future will not come either, and hence the success of the big oil company, because what they sell is not a real goods.

They are the spirits whose thoughts are inverted, and that is why they have to become expensalists, because the Universe is doing well and on the right path. And there are also those who correctly follow this reality of the Universe. Whereas the expensalists can spend their whole life acting in this way, and they come back convinced that only they are right. But they feed with it, a great social conflict, because those who are right will not allow themselves to snatch power, be it political or economic, and give it to the expensalists, because those who are not expensalists understand that the expensalists will not know how to handle the situation.

But anyway, it is good to observe, that this superficial attitude of the expensalists, are the actions that enrich, so to speak, and further strengthen the criteria of those spirits that can think correctly.

Perhaps what works best to get the expensalist out of his or her world is hypnosis, as long as the psychologist or hypnotist does not have the same expensalist bias, because I know several psychologists who have it. In such a way, that those who wish to direct the hypnosis, have to be those who really know how to point it, in order to identify these people, who little by little will be the ones who allow themselves to be led to the reality, that the world can be seen from other perspectives, or that in the world, there are many poor people, who have to be helped, so that every good acquired has a greater value, and only in this way will it be possible to obtain the sincere flattery that the expensalists look for.

But some will have observed that these people are taken into account, but after we have incurred a great insistence. However, after what was agreed in the morning, in the afternoon they forgot it and fall back into their state of mistrust, because they are undecided. And they will continue to ponder towards a void; or convinced, that the world is just as they see it. And that for them, the wrong ones are the others. So we really have to have what many call patience to be able to interact with the expensalists.

And the expensalists will have to climb upwards to reach a transition point, just as water molecules turn into steam from the surface of a pond.

But paradoxically, despite not being able to occupy the highest positions, many times the humblest are the most faithful. And they are in number as the water that remains liquid in the pond; and they are the most obedient who contribute the most to the noble cause; for example of a church, or in a government; and they are the ones who support the church or government with more strength and dedication. But the expensalists with their skill also deceive, and many humble people fervently defend the expensalists. Perhaps because they don't know, or because they are also expensalists who hope that someday they too will be able to occupy those high positions.

2

IN POLITICS, OPPOSITION IS NOT TO OPPOSE

The expensalism is what helps to create a resentful collective injustice, and from there arise the great social conflicts that will never end; until a single caste of conscious and intelligent Beings is formed. And to achieve this, we need to form a new society, so that, at the same time, a new humanity is formed both physically and energetically.

And the expensalists call to the democrat as dictator, because they speak of freedom, but to own their freedom to oppress others. And if they were poor, but managed to get out of a state of poverty, then they will despise those who are still poor. And with their accumulated fortunes, the expensalists seek out and pay well to other expensalists, in order to achieve their goals, and expand their dominion over others. And so will be kept alive a great conflict that never ends, because it is fueled by an unlawful act that causes a perennial struggle be-tween two different classes. But this struggle will only end when there is only one social class.

And Bertrand Russel said: "The problem with the world, is that the inept ones are sure of everything, while the capable live full of doubts".

But the world, and everyone's great concern, is that these expensalist "thinkers" have been the cause of the greatest tragedy, which has caused the division of the human race. And everything happened, from the moment the knowledge fell into the hands of the expensalists, and they saw the opportunity to make an economic profit. That is, in the hands of those who absorb knowledge from others, to use it only for perverse actions, or with the sole objective of earning money by selling their lethal armaments. But with it, they drag and sweep, together as a *vademecum* with that tragedy, all living beings, towards one of the greatest misfortunes that any civilization has caused on Earth.

And the expensalists love politics, because participating in politics gives them the opportunity to rule, and their orders can be obeyed by a collective. And there is a great opportunity to give a speech; or to handle a false rhetoric with great skill, because they can walk from one side to the other to boast, and be able to show off their oratorial talents, by means of a harangue that they learned, but they could not imagine it, because they do not have in their mind, as expensalists, any traced objective. And if they do not achieve it, but they have a lot of money, because they acquired it through corruption, they can influence to generate a national conflict, but using lies, to hide by means of blackmail, the origin of its decomposition.

But they do not plan a reasonable strategy, for example to win votes in a game where democratic norms and the rule of law prevail. Because as science overshadows religions, humanity must necessarily create the rules that govern coexistence; but these rules must be respected by all, so that a society can coexist. But the expensalists, generally apply a strategy the other way around, to get the votes. And they only live in the moment they are due, without being able to go from left to right the panorama of events. That is to say, that the expensalists lack a future or imaginary vision; of mental acuity and they are only venters as dogs. They don't plan mentally, because they can't have imagination; therefore, they can't be visionaries either, so as to be able to imagine what it will be like or how to get to what a society wants to be. And they walk with the toes of their feet, because they want to appear to be different from others.

Also in this case of politics, the expensalists are the ones who cause the great social conflicts, because the expensalists cause a great social discontent; since they lack a rooting, a loyalty towards themselves, so they do not care about a political distinction. So they can be in government without agreeing with the government, because they will only be on the side that determines the care of their interests. In other words, expensalists on either side are shameless. And from there, they participate on one side or the other, regardless of the motives or the reasons for the social struggles.

And in order to resolve these uncertainties, the real leaders, who can have and bring a strategy to redirect and reorder all that conflict caused by the expensalists, present themselves or arrive. Even these leaders don't care about money, and they don't assign any value to their fortunes, no matter how big they may be, as Simón Bolívar did. Or as I'm writing this, I just got an email from the Bill & Melinda Gates Foundation, which means that you also have to recognize Bill Gates' generosity to want to share his fortune through a foundation that serves mainly children and sick people with low resources.

But once the expensalists see that the leader has managed to re-establish order, they will try again to take over the administration; because they think, and are completely sure, that they are the best ones, and the only ones who can do it better. And if all is well, they understood that opposition is to oppose, and they damage everything, because somehow, they are the only ones who can do things well. And they will resort to all sorts of tricks or deceptions, to make the world see that it is the fault of the one who did things right. Because they are the expensalists who know everything. And this may seem like a parody to fill in this book, but it turns out that it's a real situation, and it's what feeds the conflicts between human beings.

In some countries, it is erroneously called government, the group of people who manage the resources of the State. And, the correct name is administration. And government means the group that manages. But the sense of meaning has been taken as someone who bullies or intimidates with a whip of command.

But the word opposition is not to oppose either, because in politics, what is meant by the word opposition, or its true meaning, is that the administration or management in turn, does things better than the previous management. In such a way that it obliges the voters, so that they can choose the best, or that they choose correctly the one who proves to them, that they can better manage the resources that belong to all.

But many understand that opposition is to oppose, and turn to opposing ideas as real expensalists. In other words, they speak badly of the one who is currently directing the administration, using strategies based on lies and offenses. Or they hide basic goods, such as food and medicine, in an attempt to bend the majority. And what they believe the other administration did well, then they try to destroy it, because the idea of the expensalists, is to oppose everything, in order to capture the admiration and vote of 50% of the population that is also expensalist.

Or they resort to strategies that are only psychological in nature, such as hatred and xenophobia, in an attempt to gain admiration. But they always want to win. And if this doesn't work for them, then they turn to other expensalists, who also have a lot of weapons and money, because these expensalists have managed to better protect what they acquired as expensalists. This induced hatred assures their domination, but it is already in an uncontrollable or global way, because as we said, the expensalists do not have borders, and they can deploy their domains and ambitions, since they cannot foresee the great harm they cause to humanity. Because they don't really know it, because they are expensalists.

But as they love politics, they do not undertake a scientific career, but a profession in which it is not necessary to think much. And scientists don't want to know anything about politics, because they are only intoxicated by science.

And the expensalists are not able to understand that opposition does not really mean to oppose, but to do things better than the other administration. For example, if one administration builds 5 schools, and the other that is not expensalist opposes it from the turn of its administration; and to oppose it, the one that is not expensalist builds, instead of 5 schools, 10 schools; in order to do so, demonstrate that he is a better administrator, or that he has the capacity to know that the best

way to lead a nation, is for its population to be educated, because of this positive opposition, now the nation will have instead of 5, 15 schools.

But when the administration's turn is for an expensalist, we will
have zero schools, because as an expensalist, he opposes, and
does not build any school. And since he was not the one who
built the 5 schools, the expensalist believes that the best way
to make an opposition is to destroy the 5 schools that the
other administration built. And there won't be any more
schools, because he didn't attend them, since he didn't build
them, and therefore managed to destroy them. Now the nation in addition to zero schools, will have a hundred works
rendered unusable by the expensalists.

And the expensalists hide between one administration and the
other, causing great damage to both administrations, and
they can, for example, create hyperinflation, because as expensalists, their only hope is to become millionaires, but it
doesn't matter that with those millions they can't buy anything, because the expensalists don't know that the value of
all goods is relative. But they are only expensalists. And since
the relative value of the goods affects the purchasing power
of the majority, mainly that of the poorest, of course the expensalists believe that this is the right way for them to become
the administrators again.

And the expensalists, squander the resources of the nations,
because they do not know how to administer them, but they
believe, that they are the government; but not with the correct
term of managers, but that they can persecute or intimidate
with their punishment. And as much as they can, they destroy

it, and have no other case than to hand over the administration. But when the other administration arrives and manages to put everything back in order, they want to take over the administration by force. And if they do it in a legal way, then they will destroy again what the new administration managed to put in order; even hatred can be so high that they attack and destroy, something that makes no sense as it is, that of ramming against the ornament.

And this seems to be like a story made up to be blamed on a certain administration, but it is really what causes the great failure of a civilization that manages to self-destruct. Once, for example, I had the opportunity to observe an administrator who managed to put a great nation in order. He did not intervene in wars. And in the transfer of command, the outgoing administrator gave the incoming administrator some books, where it was specified, and he told him so, that he gave him a surplus of 750,000 million dollars. But the new administrator, as an expensalist, wanted to give that account, but the only thing he saw were wars, and caused the great nation a deficit of 750 billion dollars. In other words, the expensalist, as the new head of that administration, caused an expense to that nation of 1,500,000 million dollars. But in addition, he left his country plunged into a war against all. He left the world as a battlefield. And a civilization with those characteristics, truly that will not be able to sustain itself for long.

But another of the most regrettable things is that precisely, we will not know if these expensalists will ever realize that they are expensalists. Well, as we have already said, it is like trying to explain to a madman the origin of his madness. Or because the energy-body connection is not always going to happen as expected; and in some there is great confusion in this regard.

But in the opposite case, if we meet or come across someone who is not an expensalist but a leader, one is immersed in a true empathy, with those people who see things from the same point of view. And not by chance, these great friends are from the same profession. Such as musicians, for example, or those euphoric religious congregations. And because expensalism is relative, even if they show that desire collectively, many times when they are left alone, the expensalists return to their condition. But not without first, convinced that they are the ones who deserve to occupy the highest positions in the church. And if they do not succeed, then they found their own church apart.

Some make the ranks in the church unreachable by the common, because the highest offices keep them under absolute zeal and secrecy. And as for a government, there form impenetrable circles of power. For these seats are reserved for the most honorable; and they yield it only to those who are more expensalists; or in a church, to those who contribute socially and economically to "the noble cause of their church". But they make sure in some way to be the life pastors, and stay at the top of the pyramid, so they will never abandon their first place. It is thought that the wars of the Middle East are nourished, because when a prophet died, he did not leave a successor in his place.

But if it were a nation governed by expensalists, they elaborate laws that preserve only their interests, and place in the key positions of the administration, other expensalists of confidence, such as the Minister of Finance, the Head of the Treasury, or the President of the Central Bank. And they will be life posts, because they take care that these key points are not subject to a voting process. And with their laws, they exempt themselves from their crimes; or even provide for them. Because even if they don't commit crimes, because they are supposed to, the expensalists only see crimes, wars and enemies everywhere in their empty minds. And in this forward-looking way, that fear makes them foresee the punishment of those crimes before committing them, because they are already prepared, or if necessary. Because in their minds, there is only the cautious defense of their interests, if someone dared to take them away. And they form a true monarchy.

And the great world conflicts are created only by the expensalists of the Earth. But the most circumspect problem would be to know, why do human beings act that way? And this book could be more extensive, but the idea is that it should be a summary of the eight previous books, because humanity, truly that it cannot continue along this path of expensalism, but it has to be a very pleasant and joyful coexistence among all the beings that inhabit the Earth.

ABOUT THE AUTHOR

GRADUATED FROM THE SCHOOL OF CHEMISTRY, FACULTY OF SCIENCES OF THE CENTRAL UNIVERSITY OF VENEZUELA, WITH A DEGREE IN CHEMICAL TECHNOLOGY. POSTGRADUATE STUDIES IN FOOD SCIENCE AND TECHNOLOGY. SPECIAL WORK ON THE CHEMISTRY OF NATURAL PRODUCTS AND THE CHEMISTRY OF DISEASES. STUDY OF COSMOLOGY AND THE ORIGIN OF SPIRITUAL ENERGY.

EXPENSALISM

www.ingramcontent.com/pod-product-compliance
Lightning Source LLC
Chambersburg PA
CBHW021549290526
45784CB00016B/2749